Financial Management

The Ultimate Guide to Planning, Organizing, Directing, and Controlling the Financial Activities of an Enterprise

Contents

Introduction

Whether you are running a social enterprise with just two full-time staff, an Internet start-up, a craft business on Etsy or a Fortune 500 multinational, you will need to have a good feel for financial management to get the best out of it.

You might manage to run your business adequately without budgets – if you have got a great product or you've got more than enough work as a consultant – but to take the next step up, or to manage in a tougher economic environment, you really need to manage your finances better.

This book is here to help.

Whether you are a small business owner, or a senior manager in another discipline who needs to brush up on financial concepts, we have aimed to explain finance simply and with plenty of real-life examples that make it easy to see how to apply the concepts in practice. We have also concentrated on what the financial figures mean, and how to figure out the message they are sending, rather than on how to construct a balance sheet or do an audit. Many trained accountants focus on the 'right answers' rather than reading between the lines to see what is going on – this book takes the opposite approach.

For instance, looking at the ratios might be your first advanced warning that you are pricing your jobs too keenly to win business, and you need to rein back and think a bit more about how to maintain your margins. Alternatively, if you are making a significant margin, and it is still rising, you might think about that as a resource you can use. Would a discount offer or a pay for referrals campaign be a good way to use that margin as a way to get new business? It is not the figures so much as thinking *beyond* the figures that can really help you make better business decisions.

You should also think about having a basic business dashboard. When you drive a car, you get various indicators on the dashboard. The speedometer is the big one, but it will also show you stuff you need to check from time to time. For example, how full is the tank? Some financial figures you need to have at the front of your mind, like the speedo, while others you can check less often – which ones will depend on your function and the type of business you are running.

Build your key stats into a single page display using charts or infographics so you can *see* what is going on. Here are some examples:

• One small business owner has an unusual approach. She works merely to pay her medical insurance and basic household bills. Then she travels to music festivals the rest of the year. Her dashboard simply shows days worked and money earned with a forecast of how many more days she needs to work to hit the target. Oddly enough, the date of Burning Man is also prominently displayed with a forecast of whether she will hit that date or not.

• A retailer gets his accountants to produce a report that shows, at the top, total sales comparisons against the last three years, and a gross margin comparison. Beneath, he can see fixed costs and the level by which monthly operating profit exceeds them. He is focused on increasing sales – if they drop, he immediately investigates why, and takes action – and on keeping gross margins constant – again, if margins drop, he investigates the mix of product that is going out of the door. However, his accountants have just suggested another chart at the bottom of the page – how fast stock is turning over. That will show if he has unfashionable or obsolescent product lines that aren't selling.

• An architect's office has a display that focuses on how much of the team's total working hours capacity is utilized and how much pay they are getting billed per hour.

Building your dashboard is something very few finance books will tell you to do, but it is one of the most important factors in making your business more successful. Moreover, the key is that you have to do it yourself – or in partnership with your finance people – because only you know your priorities and the figures that will help you focus on them.

If you have built a useful dashboard, you've also built a presentation that you can show your bankers and investors, so that it can do double service. Financial management can help grow your business. It can also help protect it. In a recession, many firms will see their revenues take a dive. Some just cut everything they can; they close plants or offices, and cut jobs or put employees on short time, on a flat percentage across the firm. Others take a look at the numbers first; they look for the products that aren't contributing much in margin, they look at capacity that is underutilized and think about whether they can use it more efficiently, and they look at what areas of the business are holding up best.

It is not surprising that the firms with the best information and the best plans tend to be the firms that stay in the game.

You also need to manage your finances – and this, too, can make the difference between surviving and thriving, or surviving and going under.

We will teach you how to look at business funding and working capital, and how to manage your business' finances to fund growth and to make your business more stable in the long term. You may be doing this yourself, or you may need to hire a finance, treasury, or credit control manager to do parts of this for you, depending on the size of your business.

Then, of course, there is the matter of getting your accounts in order and getting them audited. You know what? Any accountant can do that. That is not really what this book is about – it's about making your business better and stronger.

Chapter 1 – What Is Financial Management and Why Do You Need It?

Financial management is about money. It is about controlling, monitoring, planning, and directing the use of funds in an organization. Whatever has to do with finance, from the petty cash tin to a billion-dollar public offering of shares, is part of financial management's remit. Unless you plan to pay your staff nothing, charge nothing for your products and services, and have no assets, you will need finance somewhere in the organization. And you'll need to manage it. So really, there is no escape from financial management – if you ask "why do I need it?" you might as well ask "why do I need to breathe?" or "why do I need to eat?" You just do!

On the other hand, why do you need *good* financial management?

• Because if you don't have good financial systems, you are not fully in control of your business. Imagine two beer festivals, both running for a week. One has a report of how much beer has sold within fifteen minutes of closing. The other doesn't record what has sold. Which one do you think has the more chance of running out of beer without having reordered? Which one has the higher chance that it will end up with a lot of wastage?

• Many start-ups have a tough time when they want to raise funds for growth. They have been going for a couple of years, but venture capitalists or bankers want to see figures that break down their activities in greater detail – and they don't have them. Or the figures they do have are somewhat approximate. It makes life much, much easier if you have good financial management from the start.

• Good financial systems let you make smart budgets. Instead of just trying to increase all sales or cut all costs, good systems will help you identify those areas where you can make the most impact.

• Good financial systems let you see how you are doing. If margins take a dive, or if your sales in one area are running away, you can see straight away, and take corrective action, or divert more resources to support your success.

• Good financial systems help 'police' your business. You will see how well each branch is doing, and you can see if something is going wrong, whether that's a simple mistake (one retailer caught a store where a member of staff had managed to print out all the $99 labels as $9.99!) or theft or fraud.

• Good financial management will help you make sure your business is well capitalized and has the right financial structure. For instance, if you deal with long contracts and project payments that can stretch several years into the future, you need to have a good equity base and long-term financing – or, perhaps, you could look into trade finance. Otherwise, you are going to find your finances stretched whenever you have outgoings, but none of your projects are reaching milestones this month.

• Good financial management makes sure your customers aren't taking advantage of you. Too many businesses have been forced into bankruptcy when a big customer goes bust and hasn't paid its bills. A well-thought-out credit control policy, together with good reporting systems, should flag up any issues before they become critical.

A great product or service is a wonderful thing. However, a great *business* has to add more to the mix. It has to add marketing, of course, so that customers get to know about the product and want to buy it. But it also has to add financial management, so that the business is supported by financial resources, and can put those resources to the best use.

You won't *start* a business by applying financial management. However, it is financial management that keeps it healthy and growing.

So... let's get on with learning about the basics of finance: the financial statements.

Chapter 2 – Financial Statements

If you have ever looked at an annual report from a big company, you will have noticed how it splits into different sections. There are pretty pictures and (usually) optimistic words at the front, and then there is a boring black and white section with the numbers. There are numbers in the front section, too, but usually arranged in infographics, and selected to give the best impression.

If you want the truth, better look at the boring bits and do your own calculations – that is how great investors get to grips with the companies they invest in.

If you can grab an annual report to look at while you are using this book, you will make your life much easier – and you'll be learning from a real-world example, which will help you when you come to apply the lessons to your own business. You may be able to order one up from a major company or download a pdf from the Internet. It is easier to start on a manufacturing, services or retail business, like Intel, Microsoft or Amazon, rather than a bank or insurance company, as the latter has a specific type of business that is not so easy to understand.

There are three principal statements to looks at.

First, there is the profit and loss account – how much money the company is making.

Second, there is the balance sheet – what the company owns and what it owes.

And third, there is the cash flow account, and this adjusts the profits to show what cash actually came into and went out of the company.

Let's think of that in terms of a typical household:

• The profit and loss account shows your salary coming in, your various bills being paid out, and what is left at the end of the month for savings.

• The balance sheet shows the value of your car, house, designer handbags, Star Wars figurine collection, whatever – *less* the total of your mortgage, personal loans, and credit card balance.

• The cash flow account adjusts the profit and loss account to show actual cash in and out. For instance, if you buy a car for cash, your profit and loss account should show the depreciation on the car every month over its expected useful life, but the cash flow will show the actual purchase price in the month you buy it. The idea is that the profit and loss account smooths out investment decisions like buying a car or a factory – but the cash flow shows only cash.

The Profit and Loss Account

The profit and loss account is, in essence, a series of subtractions. We start with the revenue of the business – its total sales (or rents, or royalties) – and then we subtract the costs to arrive at the profit.

We so often talk in generic terms about 'making a profit' or 'the company's profits', but one of the things we need to think about is that there are several levels of profit.

There is *gross profit* – that is a return on materials cost before you take any other costs (like premises, staff or finance) into account. Retailers work on gross margin – or invert the ratio to work on 'markup'. They buy a crate of apples at $45 and need to sell at, say, a 100% markup, or $90. You *can* also look at gross profit in services – if you are selling billable hours. It is the difference between what you pay your staff and what you sell their time for (though you would need to exclude non-billable hours and support staff from the equation).

If you look at all the operating costs of a business, including the premises costs (rent, electricity, depreciation of machinery, etc.), support staff, professional fees, and so on, what you get when you subtract them from the revenues of the business is the *operating profit*. It is a good level at which to look at the profitability of operations overall, as it doesn't matter whether your business is entirely equity funded, or financed mainly by bank loans – the operating profit will be the same.

Next, we subtract the financial costs of the business. So if you have any bank loans or mortgages, this is where you take out the servicing cost for the period that we are looking at, whether it is a month, quarter or year. All the interest paid is subtracted (and if you are lucky enough to have a pot of cash, of course, it is added back in). Here we have *pre-tax profit*.

Next, we take out tax. In a perfect world, it would be the tax rate times the pre-tax profit – but because the tax department has different rules about what is an allowable expense from the accountants, it will often differ a bit from what you would expect. *Post-tax profit* is profit free and clear, and now you can decide what to do with it. If you are a one-person business, it is all yours; if you're running a company, you have to decide whether to pay a dividend to shareholders.

Take out the dividend, or whatever you took out for yourself, and what you have left is *retained profit* – the profit for the year that is left in the business to fund future investment. Some businesses keep all the profit – that is a good decision if you know you can invest at a rate of return higher than the bank pays on cash. For instance, if you are in a fast-growing business. That is why many tech companies don't pay dividends.

Remember we talked about how the profit and loss account is different from the cash flow? One big item that is different is *amortization and depreciation.* When you buy a long-term business asset, you estimate how long it will last – a computer might last three years, a major piece of manufacturing equipment twenty years. If you are going to use a bread oven for 15 years, then you say 'Okay, every year I'm going to use 1/15 of the oven, so to speak, so I'm going to match the 1/15 of the cost of the oven with the revenues each year to find my profit' – in accountant-speak, you amortize the cost over 15 years (you might also reckon that if you are likely to sell the oven for scrap at the end, you should take the scrap value as a *residual value...* but that is a level of detail we don't need to worry about).

Anyway, we might want to add back that depreciation and amortization. The difference? Depreciation is on physical objects, amortization on intangibles, like goodwill and software. We will add it back to get a better idea of the cash profit that the business is making – and we add it back to the operating profit to get EBITDA, earnings before interest, tax, depreciation, and amortization. That is a great number that a lot of businesses use for benchmarking because however a business is funded, and whatever its asset base, EBITDA will compare well across the industry. (Besides, one firm might think your bread oven's only good for ten years – so for every $100 you charge in depreciation, that firm would be charging $150. Suppose you had the same revenues and the same costs, apart from depreciation – that company would look less profitable on every measure except for EBITDA, which would be exactly the same.)

The Balance Sheet

Where the profit and loss account works on the basis of subtraction, the balance sheet is about addition. You add up all the assets of the business – the things you own. Then you add up all the liabilities of the business – things you owe to others (that includes bank loans, but also services you have to provide for which you've already been paid, trade invoices you haven't paid, and a provision for tax you will pay next year on profit you made this year). Each side of the balance sheet should balance – that's how it gets its name.

But why does it balance?

Let's just think about a very simple business. Suppose you kick off with $100 in cash which you decide to invest in setting up a little crafts business selling on Etsy. You spend $50 on a sewing machine and $20 on textiles, and then you make some nice tote bags. Your balance sheet has one liability – $100 that is owed to you, in shareholder's equity; and it has three assets – the sewing machine, the cloth, and $30 in cash. That is why it balances.

You sell all of your original stock for $50, and for the sake of simplicity, we are going to decide you don't pay yourself anything. So now your asset side shows $50 for a sewing machine, no textiles (all gone), and $80 in cash – the $30 you had, and the $50 that customers paid. That is $130 against the original $100.

However, you have made a profit, don't forget – $50 less the $20 you paid for the cloth. That profit belongs to shareholders (let's ignore tax for the moment), that is, to you – so you have to add it to the liabilities side of the balance sheet. $100 plus the $30 profit equals $130, and hey presto, both sides of the balance sheet balance, all over again.

Suppose you decide to borrow $100 from the bank. Now you have $230 on the liabilities side, consisting of $130 in equity and retained profit plus $100 debt. But the money you have borrowed will sit on the assets side as $100 cash, or as the value of whatever assets you've bought with the money. So, again, the balance sheet balances.

The balance sheet is useful for looking at the business' resources, both physical and financial. For instance, you can look at the tangible assets – how much money have you invested? And how productively is it being put to use? How much stock or work in progress have you got?

You can also look at your sources of funding – how much is debt? How much is equity? How much retained profit do you have? (that is the amount that you can distribute in dividends, so it is a more important number than it might seem).

You can look at the balance between long-term and short-term assets, and whether your funding sources match it – if you have a lot of long-term assets, but your financing is all short-term (like an overdraft), you might want to think about restructuring your balance sheet.

We are going to look at the ratios that can help you analyze these statements further in a later chapter. For now, just get happy with the format of these accounts and, if you like, track down the detail in the notes to the accounts, which will show you what has gone into each overall category.

Actually, the notes to the accounts are where real finance nerds get their fun. Very, very occasionally you might find that the numbers don't add up! Over the years, analysts have found various bodies buried in the notes:

• An investment in shares in a company that then became a client and bought its shareholder's software – they couldn't get customers any other way!

• A big leasing company that looked as if it was making loads of profit – but if you did the cash flow sums correctly, was hemorrhaging cash.

• A company that was capitalizing all its marketing costs, 'saving' millions a year.

• A company that everyone thought was a house builder, but when you looked at the detailed breakdowns of revenue, made more money trading building plots.

• The use of special purpose vehicles to hide huge amounts of debt (Enron).

• Large payments to directors of the company including loans to directors which were never repaid.

• Special purpose vehicles used to create paper profits when the parent company 'sold' them supplies or charged them interest on loans.

Some pieces of creative accounting don't come to light until the company crashes and burns. However, other pieces of creative accounting are there to see – if you trawl deep enough.

You may not, right now, be up to it, but you can get an idea of what goes on by reading *The Smartest Guys in the Room* or *Conspiracy of Fools* (about Enron), or *The Big Short* (about the sub-prime mortgage bubble, though this is more finance markets than company finance), or *Final Accounting* (Arthur Andersen, the accountancy firm that fell apart after its role in the Enron collapse came to light).

Chapter 3 – Looking At Cash Flow

As we mentioned, the profit and loss statement makes various adjustments which don't match the actual movement of cash in the business. If you are in a cash business, you might not be too worried – sell a punnet of strawberries, and get $3 back, ring up the sale on the till and you're done. But suppose you are a contractor who has to pay electricians, carpenters, and plasterers to refurbish a house, and you get paid at the end of the work, and you even give your customers 30 days to pay after they are invoiced – you will book the sale when you send the invoice, but your cash goes out a long time ahead of the sale, and you don't get cash when you invoice, only afterwards.

All businesses above a certain size will produce a cash flow account as part of their audited figures. But even if you don't have to, it is worth doing a cash flow account to see what's going on in the business – in fact, some small businesses operate on a cash accounting basis from the start. Remember that the P&L is designed to show the money the business makes in a particular period, but it is designed to match revenues and costs – for instance, by capitalizing an asset and then depreciating it over time, rather than taking all the purchase price out of the P&L at once – while the cash flow account shows the money that has actually come in and gone out, whatever it relates to.

Here are a few of the fundamental differences between the profit and loss account and the cash flow:

• *Capitalization of Costs* – as we have seen, when you buy a major asset like a manufacturing plant or a vehicle, the cost is 'capitalized' – the asset is put into the balance sheet and depreciated every year of its life, matching the cost of the asset to the revenues it generates (this matching is called the 'accruals basis').

Some companies also capitalize costs like research and development, or own-developed software. They might also capitalize their internal costs of commissioning a new plant. For instance, the time staff put into installing the new plant, delivery costs, the cost of hiring an engineer to calculate the load on the factory floor... From the point of view of the cash flow account, though, if those costs have been paid for in real money, it is cash flow going out.

• *Depreciation and Amortization (which we have already talked about)* – they are taken as costs in the P&L, but they're not 'real' cash.

• *Working Capital* – if you give your customers credit, your revenue isn't all cash. If you don't pay your suppliers on the nail, again, you have got costs in the profit and loss account that aren't 'real'. The cash flow account recognizes the changes in working capital over the year.

For instance, if you invested in a huge campaign to get new customers and let them have extra special credit terms for their first order, your receivables would have increased, which is a use of your funds. You need to adjust profits downwards to take account of the fact you haven't been paid yet.

• *Timing Differences* – dividends are declared for the year and shown in the P&L for that year – but they are actually paid to shareholders in the financial year that comes afterwards. Tax is similar – the liability is shown in the P&L, but what is shown in cash flow is the tax you paid on *last* year's profits. (Take care when you are doing monthly accounts. Advance payments need to be apportioned to the right time periods in the P&L – for instance, your annual insurance payment or professional membership all go out in one cash payment, but is 'accrued' with 1/12 of the cost shown in the P&L for each month of the year; so these have to be adjusted back again for the cash flow.)

• *Money Coming in From Funding Sources* – if you issue new shares for cash, that is shown in the balance sheet but not the profit and loss account, so it needs to be added to the cash flow statement.

The difference between cash flow and profit is one reason that apparently profitable, high growth companies sometimes hit the buffers. 'Overtrading' occurs when a company is having to grant credit to increasing numbers of new customers but has to pay its suppliers from the smaller cash flow that is coming in from past sales. Good financial management will ensure that there is adequate finance to support the new higher level of sales. However, the effect can be particularly savage when a young company finds its suppliers have put it on very short credit terms, says 15 or 30 days, while customers are paying only in 120 days. The company may look profitable, but it is getting squeezed on cash flow.

Equally, some companies look as if they are not making much profit, but their cash flow position is better than it looks. For instance, travel agents and tour operators are often paid upfront by customers booking summer vacations months ahead and don't have to pay costs till later, so they are awash with cash for much of the year – if they get their financial management right. That lets them survive on slimmer margins than they would otherwise need.

Chapter 4 – Forecasting, Budgeting, and Flex

When you look at the financial statements of a public company, you are looking at a historical statement of what happened last year. As a business owner or an investor, you are more concerned by what is going to happen in future, and you're going to want some way of checking that things are turning out according to plan. That is why we have forecasting and budgets. But just doing forecasts and budgets isn't enough – you have to use them tactically.

For instance, at one firm, managers of a small but thriving business unit were *stopped* from making more sales because there wasn't the budget to handle distribution of the product. Someone, somewhere, needed to take a look at the budgets and work out how to finance the unexpectedly successful line of sales – instead of which the company choked off the growth of its new product.

We are going to take a look at ways you can make sure your budgets keep up with reality.

If you are already in business and you have a couple of years' accounts, budgeting is relatively easy. You probably have a good feel for your costs, and you have a reasonable feel for sales. However, even if you are a start-up, you ought to at least try to forecast a level of sales. Whether that is by estimating how many customers you can get interested and what you might make out of each one or by estimating how many cupcakes you can bake and hoping you can sell 90% of them each day, or by looking at what a competitor makes and thinking about how much of the market you can grab off them.

Let's look at a few different start-ups:

• Frederique knows her unit materials cost and pricing very well. She makes flutes, and each one costs her $80 in wood. She knows from what is in the market that she can charge $400 a flute and still be very competitive. However, she doesn't know how many she can sell. She can build a basic budget using $320 as her gross profit, and the big variable will be units. Next year, once she has worked out how many she can sell, she will have a better idea what she can pay herself. Good thing she has a day job as a teacher!

• Henry is setting up a pizza delivery service. He knows there is one a few blocks away and has worked out, by looking at the riders going out over the last few weeks, what he thinks it's making in revenues. He knows what the riders are paid, and he has already worked out his premises costs. His big decisions are marginal – whether to compete on a lower price or spend a bit more on materials and go for the Generation X 'foodies' as customers.

• Tom's new printing operation has a huge fixed cost covering its premises and presses, and staff who are graphic designers. He has paid for it all out of his own pocket and reckons he has enough funding to pay for about eight months of operations before breaking. The budget has been designed to feed in the right amount of business to cover fixed costs within the first six months giving him a small margin of error. However, that is still quite tight – so Tom decides to borrow from the bank so that he can do more advertising to the target customer base and try to grow the business faster. It is a risk – but not as risky as potentially not being able to cover the costs.

As you can see, budgeting isn't a one-size-fits-all process. You need to think about the priorities of the business, the balance between fixed costs and variable (per-unit) costs, and also which of the figures are relatively certain (usually costs, but you might even have subscriptions or long-term contracts which give you reasonably certain elements of revenue), and which estimates are sketchier.

Another exercise which is useful is to look at what discretion you have over a particular figure:

- *Pricing* – do you have to accept the market level of pricing, or do you have flexibility? Is demand elastic (so higher prices will shrink your volume of sales) or inelastic (customers will pay for reliability or brand)?

Taking the example of Henry's pizza parlor, he has some flexibility depending on the market he is aiming for – if he goes for the 'foodie' market he can get prices 50% higher than otherwise, but he has to think about whether he is losing some volume of business with that strategy.

- *Input Costs* – for instance, if Henry goes low-cost, he could buy cheaper mozzarella, he could adjust recipes to use less of the high-cost ingredients, like Parma ham, and use more (cheap) tomato sauce. But he probably can't do much about the cost of firing the oven, or the cost of rent once he is up and running – though he needs to do some investigation to make sure he gets a reasonable real estate deal in the first place.

- *Volume of Sales* – you may think that is just up to the customers, but there's quite a lot you can do to affect the figure, such as discount offers or short-term marketing campaigns.

A larger business will have several different levels of budgets. There will be a master budget for the entire enterprise, but underneath that there will be subsidiary budgets relating to each part of the business – a financial budget, operating budgets for each line of business, capital expenditure budgets and perhaps program budgets for particular areas of work. Many of those budgets will be linked, and obviously, managing the budgets across the business is a detailed and time-consuming job.

Generally, budgets are set for the year and then divided up into monthly budgets. Be aware of seasonality when you are doing this – for instance, any shop that sells stationery knows that you get a huge amount of trade when the new school year starts. That is the cue for parents and students to lay in stocks of exercise books, folders, pens, and so on. To account for that, your budgets should be made to allow higher stock purchasing and holding over the preceding month and a half, and higher sales in the first month of the new school year. (If you don't buy in extra stock, you risk not being able to meet demand when it arrives.)

Budgets need to be regularly monitored – usually each month. This used to be a big job for the accountant, but if you have a spreadsheet you can set it up to be almost automatic – accounting software also automates comparisons.

You are looking for various comparisons:

• Actual against budget – did you achieve what was expected, or do better or worse?

• Actual against last month

• Actual against last year (both month to corresponding month, and Year-To-Date)

It is easy to think that having higher revenue or lower costs is 'good', but you need to be a bit more thoughtful than that to get the best out of budgeting. If revenue is higher, look for the reasons – for instance, was there one big order carried over from last month? Was there a major event that influenced sales?

For example, if I was running a sports bar and my revenue was up 5%, I might think I was doing well – but if the Football World Cup was on, and my revenue was *only* up 5%, I would actually be doing a very poor job of converting that to revenue. (Euro 2016 saw beer sales up 8% every match day.)

You also need to track the relation between different items. For instance, if your sales have increased, costs that relate directly to sales should have increased by the same amount (or more, if you used promotional offers such as buy-one-get-one-free to achieve the revenue increase).

Having looked at how the business is doing, you then need to take action. Remember, a budget is a tool – it shouldn't manage the business. If you find that you keep bumping up against budget constraints, you need to do some hard thinking. Maybe the business has grown faster than expected – it could be time to redraft the budget to allow the business to take on more staff, or purchase more inventory.

When you look at your budget, keep your business mission and values in mind. If you want to be the top-quality player in your field, it is no good trying to skimp and save on input costs if that damages the quality of your product. Remember, a budget is a tool – just like the speedometer and revs counter in a racing driver's car.

Flexing Your Budget Muscles

It is essential that you should have a flexible budget. Otherwise, you are basically tying your business down. Imagine if you said, "We won't respond to any moves by our competitors until we get to the end of the year," or "We know customers want more of our product, but we're not going to sell it till January 1st." If you let your budget be a constraint, instead of helping you run the business, that is effectively what you are doing.

That is why you need a *flexible budget*. Quite simply, it's a budget that flexes to take account of changes in the levels of activity. For instance, you may need to run your manufacturing plant longer hours some months than others to meet orders received, or to take account of seasonality. To make a flexible budget, you work out the total cost per machine hour, and then 'flex' the budget according to the number of hours worked. Depreciation, rent, energy, and supervisory costs are all included. That ensures managers can 'flex' the budget within a given range without needing to get overspends authorized.

Manufacturing is a classic case, but you can use flexible budgets in any kind of business. Suppose you are running a catering service, and you're told one of your customers need twenty more meals a day. If you have done your sums correctly, you can simply flex the budget to increase your costs accordingly.

You should also look at cost and revenue drivers, using an approach that is called *activity-based costing*. A cost driver is the reason why a particular cost is incurred. While with variable costs – that is, costs that relate directly to the end product, like dough and cheese for pizzas – you have an easy way to allocate the cost to the product, fixed costs are more difficult to analyze.

For instance, every so often your pizza oven will need a clean-out and some maintenance. Suppose you say that you will do this every 1,000 hours and it costs you $100, then you can say that is ten cents an hour that the oven is up and running. Using ABC, you have taken an indirect (overhead) cost and linked it to a cost driver.

Using ABC will help you get more out of flex budgets. It is also a really good way to think about costs, as you are asking, basically, "Why do we do this? What's the business reason for this cost?"

Once you have started thinking that way, you might like to look at *zero-based budgeting*. Basically, you go back to first principles and look at the budgets as if the business doesn't yet exist – as if you were putting together a start-up. Every expense has to be justified – you can't just decide to increase everything by 10% on last year. So you start from what you are trying to achieve – say, in Frederique's case, after a few years, she has a nice little business making flutes, and she decides rather than just ramping everything up a few percent, she is going to sit down and take a hard look at the budgets. Her goal will be to sell eighty flutes this year. She needs to think about electricity, machine maintenance, marketing, and direct costs:

• Step changes in direct costs can sometimes be achieved when you start zero-based thinking. To make flutes, Frederique needs wood. She has been buying ready cut wood in small lots. Now that she is making a good quantity of instruments, she realizes she can buy planks – much cheaper – and cut the wood to size when she wants to make a flute.

• Marketing is a necessary cost, but let's think about the best way to do it.

For instance, like many start-up craftspeople, Frederique has been working through Etsy and eBay and paying quite large commissions. Would setting up her own website enable her to retain more of the sales price herself? Using ABC, she can compare the price per flute sold of website work with the commission she pays now.

• Frederique looks at the workshop. Obviously, she needs electricity – but zero-based budgeting says she needs to look at how much, and what price. First of all, she realizes that she can reduce her bills by batch processing flutes rather than making each one singly – it is more efficient, and so there are fewer machine hours required. Secondly, when she looks at tariffs, she finds that there is one that suits her operating hours (evenings and weekends – she is still working full-time as a teacher) better than the flat rate she's on. So though her production is going up, she can cut her bills by 10-20%.

You may think ABC and zero-based budgets are only for big companies, but this example should give you an idea about how you can build these ideas even into a one-person business and get a return on your effort.

Another refinement of ordinary budgeting is the *rolling budget*. Instead of making the budget from January 1 to December 31, and using the last couple of months of the year to make the budget for the next year, you roll the budget a month forward every time you check a month's reported out-turn. You will always have a full year of budget ahead of you. It is efficient because you do the new month's budget at the same time as monitoring results and, if necessary, revising the budget for this year. It also gives you a better view of the road ahead, particularly in the last couple of months of your financial year.

Using Budgets Strategically

Usually, budgets are made up by each operating unit within a company, and these are added together (with a bit of horse-trading and politics) to make up the overall budget. However, you should also think about using the budgeting process strategically.

For instance, if you need to make cuts, rather than cutting 10% from every operating unit, think about cutting 20% from those that are less productive or profitable, and use that to transfer more resource to the most profitable or fastest growing areas.

You might also want to think about whether you have enough funds. If your sales are growing fast, would it be sensible to raise money to support a higher level of working capital? Could you support a higher level of sales or more profitable production if you were able to refresh your manufacturing facility?

We will go into that in more detail later, but your budget meetings are a good time to start that discussion.

Chapter 5 – Capital Spending and Discounted Cash Flow Analysis

At some point, every business will want to invest in equipment, whether that is a new car for a taxi business, a massive power plant, or a more powerful computer and drafting system for an architect's office. But how do you work out whether the investment will generate a positive return? That is where discounted cash flow analysis (DCF) comes in.

It works on the basis of the *time value of money*. If you put your cash in the bank, you will get paid interest – the longer you leave it there, the more interest you get. So if you invest money, you would expect it to pay back the least the amount you'd have gained by leaving it in the bank. Suppose you lock your $100 up for five years, and at the end of the five years, the bank pays you $120 – $100 plus $20 interest. You could look at that as a return of 20% over five years, or you could say $110 in five years' time is worth $100 now. The discounted cash flow analysis is a more sophisticated and methodologically rigorous way of doing the same kind of sums.

With DCF analysis you look at the future flow of revenues or cost savings that you will get from the investment, and *discount* them back to today's value. That gives you the *present value* (PV) of those cash flows. Next, you subtract the investment that you made from the positive cash flows to get the *net* present value (NPV). If you have got things right, it should be positive.

Let's consider a classic case: buying a second piece of manufacturing plant to double capacity. First of all, we have to work out what that piece of plant will contribute to the company's cash flow – remember we are looking at cash, so there is no depreciation to think about. Maybe in the first year, it is going to take a while to get up and running, and will start off at less than capacity – so there will be 100% of extra costs but only maybe 60% of the extra revenues to take, and it won't be very profitable.

Then as you go on, the machine runs closer to capacity and both sales and profits increase. Suppose we work out the profit forecast over five years. Then we need to discount back those values. We could use the bank interest rate – not the base rate perhaps, but what we would get on that money if we tied it up in a fixed-term account.

Alternatively, we could say we want to achieve an 8% return on our money, so we would use 8% and see what happens – that is a different way to do things, but both approaches are acceptable. Just be sure you know which you are using.

Still another rate you might consider is the weighted average cost of capital (WACC) – but that is something that typically you will only find appropriate if you are a company with external shareholders and bank debt, and generally, it's only larger companies which use this approach.

$000	Year 1	Year 2	Year 3	Year 4	Year 5
Extra cash flow	40	70	100	100	100
Discount rate at 10%	$1/1.1 =$ 0.909	$1/1.1^2 =$ 0.826	$1/1.1^3 =$ 0.75	$1/1.1^4 =$ 0.68	$1/1.1^5 =$ 0.62
Present value	36	58	75	68	62
Total present value	299				
Cost of machine	250				
Net present value	49				

This example shows how to calculate net present value. The top row summarizes the extra cash flow from the new machine. The next shows the discount rate; we used 10% here. The cash flow times the discount rate gives us the present value of the year's cash flow. Note how the discount rate is higher the further away the cash flow – or, to put it another way, cash flow that is further away is worth less now than cash flow that's close to today's date. Cash flows in year one are worth 90% of the value at the end of the year, using the 10% discount rate – by year five their present value is only 62% of their future value. Having added all the cash flows together, we subtract the cost of the machine; we don't discount that because it occurs on day one.

The net present value is a positive $49,000. That means we are going to make $49,000 more than our requirement of 10% returns. That is a good investment since it handily beats the target we set.

This calculation was pretty simple. We didn't build in any price rises or inflation, and we had a single investment – sometimes you will want to look at a phased expenditure, and then you'll need to discount the capex as well as the operating cash flows. Sometimes an investment will incur losses in the first year or two. But basically, once you have got a grasp of the way DCF analysis works, you can adapt it pretty easily to more sophisticated cases.

While DCF has traditionally been used for big physical assets – power plants, ports, or new papermaking machinery, for example – it can also be applied to intangibles. For instance, if a publisher was looking at buying another publisher's backlist, a DCF calculation could be done looking at sales of those books against the amount paid for the rights. Royalties or patents can be valued in this way.

You might also look at a big marketing investment using DCF analysis – though it is not quite as easy to be sure that an increase in sales is entirely down to that investment, of course!

Chapter 6 – Some Aspects Of Treasury Management

So far, we have looked at managing your operational finances. However, we also need to think about how you fund the business. You may think that businesses stand or fall under the leadership of the CEO, and a lot of the time that is true. But sometimes, businesses that run into trouble are saved by the simple fact that the finance officer has done a splendid job of securing the right mix of funding and managing the company's working capital tightly – and companies that would otherwise have done quite well are handicapped and even wrecked by poor capital management.

In one's personal life, it is easy to see that the guy who loses his job and has a huge mortgage and a load of credit card debt is going to get in trouble, while the one without short-term debt and with equity of 50% in his house has a better chance of surviving a period of unemployment. The same is true with companies – structuring a business' finances correctly will help it weather storms, and can also help it grow faster. The job just happens to be more complex than with personal finance.

There are quite a few trade-offs to be made, too. As so often, there are no right answers, but you will need to consider various issues. For instance, the cost of capital.

Debt is usually cheaper than equity; as a company grows, you still have to pay the same amount of interest on a loan, but equity shareholders will want a share of the increased profits you make. The trade-off is that while you are obligated to pay interest on loans, you don't have to pay shareholders anything – which means loss-making early-stage businesses can benefit from issuing shares rather than relying on debt funding.

One ratio that will help you consider your funding is the debt to equity ratio, which shows *leverage* or *gearing.* If you make a 10% return on equity, shareholders get 10%; but if you add debt, say as much again as equity, and make a 10% return on the total capital employed, shareholders can get a return of nearly double that (depending on what you pay your lenders, of course) – that is what we mean by leverage. So debt can be helpful up to a point – but it is also risky, because if the bank forecloses on a loan, it can liquidate the company, and shareholders won't get anything.

You also want to think about your overall cost of capital. WACC can be complicated to calculate, but the principle is simple; take each source of funds and the rate you Are paying for it, whether that is a short-term overdraft, long-term loan, or equity. Obviously, the cost of a loan is the interest you pay; however, calculating the return demanded by shareholders is less easy because it includes capital appreciation of the shares as well as the dividends you pay. There are various ways of calculating it, but it may be simpler just to look at the dividends or drawings, particularly in an owner-managed company. You are looking for the weighted average rate. That is the rate of return any investment needs to make in order to pay for itself.

There is also a halfway house between debt and equity, the preferred share. A preferred share has a fixed-rate dividend, which doesn't grow, as common stock dividends do. It ranks ahead of the common shareholders – if its dividend hasn't been paid, no dividends can be paid on the ordinary shares – and it also gets paid out ahead of shareholders in the event of a liquidation, though behind bank loans. Preference shares tend to pay a higher interest rate than debt, but they are sometimes a useful tool for companies who want to keep their gearing down (perhaps because of regulatory requirements) and appeal to investors who want both the security of an interest return and the possibility of price appreciation as the company grows.

 A good finance officer will make sure a business has the best mix of types of debt finance. That will involve first understanding the nature of the business – debt that is good for one kind of business may not work for another.

First of all, is the business a 'steady as she goes' kind, like a real estate investment company which gets a predictable amount of rent every month? Or is it a business which can see big swings in cash flow depending on large contracts and the achievement of project milestones?

Secondly, does the business have assets on which debt can be secured?

• Companies with significant long-term assets may find they can get reasonable rates for mortgages or loans secured on assets. Asset finance is often a good way to expand vehicle fleets, for instance.

• Companies with large amounts of inventory or receivables should look at factoring or invoice discounting. This can satisfactorily support a high level of working capital – for instance, at a retailer who needs to stock up in advance of a major sales season.

• Companies which have big swings in cash flow need to have long-term, stable debt, and lots of equity. If you pair irregular cash flow with high debts or short-term debt which is immediately foreclosable, you have an accident waiting to happen.

• Companies with stable income like subscriptions, rentals, or royalties, can afford a higher level of debt.

You should also think about whether the company needs to own particular assets. For instance, a retailer could sell its premises and rent the shop space back – a 'sale and leaseback' – to help fund expansion elsewhere. Many hotel companies don't own their hotels – they simply manage the operations and the brand.

Another aspect of treasury is *capital budgeting*. Basically, it means looking at your capital investment, your long-term investment in business assets, and working out what is the best way to deploy your capital. You may have four or five different possible projects, so you will want to work out which of them is best for the business. Discounted cash flow calculations are important, but you'll also want to look at other ratios such as the internal rate of return (IRR) and the payback period.

IRR is just DCF turned around another way. IRR is the rate of return that, used as a discount rate, gives you a DCF of exactly zero. It is a good way of comparing projects that are different sizes and may have different time frames. However, just selecting the highest IRR projects could mean you take on three small projects instead of the big one that would really transform your business – don't use IRR on its own. Look at all the different methods of evaluating your investment projects.

The payback period is simple – how long does it take for the project to earn back what you spend on it? A good example of a short payback project might be adding a waste recovery or heat recovery facility to a process – it costs little compared to the overall equipment and can earn money back quickly. On the other hand, building a major solar farm could have a payback period of more than a decade.

Capital budgeting is, in a way, a beauty contest. You have got a finite amount of prize money, and you will pick the projects that can do most for the business. You may decide you want a mixture of small, quick payback projects, and one major investment that will deliver impressive returns over the longer term. You can let go of the projects that have lower returns, or that don't make an appreciable difference because they are just too small.

Of course, your money isn't finite. If you have two really good, big, well-thought-out projects, then you might decide it is worth backing both of them. In this case, you will want to think about raising new finance, either from the bank or equity investors.

Chapter 7 – Managing Your Working Capital

Working capital management is the area that gets overlooked by most business managers – many times it is an unsung hero in the finance department who gets tasked with looking after it. But in fact, managing working capital properly is crucial to improving business performance.

Working capital is basically all the short-term capital requirements of your business.

These break down into:

• *Inventory and Work In Progress* – whether you are a retailer who needs to ensure you have dresses in each size and color for the new season or a machinery manufacturer who needs to have basic components in stock. A ceramic artist could have both inventory – pots and tiles that he has made and are available for sale – and work in progress. For instance, pots that have been fired but haven't yet been painted or glazed. He probably also has some raw materials inventory – clay and glazes or paints. Inventory can account for a big slug of a business' funds.

• *Receivables* – for any business which provides goods or services first, and invoices later, receivables can represent a major use of funds. That is particularly the case where long-term contracts are involved. If you are a small supplier dealing with larger companies, such as a farmer supplying a supermarket chain or a small specialized contractor working for major construction companies, you're quite likely to find payment terms set vastly in the big guy's favor – 120 days plus isn't uncommon.

These two items soak up your finance. They can be offset by payables – where you purchase from your suppliers but don't pay till sometime after. If you are lucky, you can have turned the raw materials into finished product and have it out of the door before you have to pay your suppliers – if you're unlucky, it is the other way around.

The simple ratios you should calculate to manage your working capital are inventory days, receivables days, and payables days. For instance, inventory days can be calculated as inventory / cost of sales x 365. It is worth checking out the norm for your sector, as inventory days can vary widely – for example, a food retailer may only have a few days' of inventory – if most things are sold fresh – while a retailer selling big-ticket items such as cars or white goods would have a much longer supply.

Add together inventory days and payables days, and subtract payables days, and you have a figure showing you your *cash cycle* – the length of time it takes you to go from converting your cash into inventory and receivables, to getting that cash back again. Obviously, it is better to have as short as a cash cycle as you can. (In fact, some food retailers may even have a negative cash cycle – they get their supplies on credit and sell for cash.)

You should monitor your working capital trends as closely as you monitor your budgets. Ensure your management of working capital isn't slipping. While you might need to build up stocks at busy times or perhaps allow a bit more customer credit if you are entering a new market or trying to expand into a new customer sector, if you see inventory or receivables days expanding without any apparent reason, you need to take action.

Growing your revenues can involve high growth in your working capital, so fast-growing businesses need to be particularly aware of what is happening in their inventory and receivables. One solution is just to get more financing, perhaps through an overdraft – but funds tied up in working capital aren't making you any money, so your business won't be as profitable as it should be. If your working capital is growing faster than your sales, and your cash cycle is expanding, then you need to get a grip and tighten up on your stocks and receivables.

Keeping Working Capital Tight

Better management of working capital can start with some very basic changes. For instance, how long does it take you to invoice a sale? Some businesses don't get around to sending invoices out for as long as four weeks. Then they send a paper invoice through the post. That is crazy – you are handing customers up to a month and a half of extra credit just by not getting your systems in order. Organize electronic invoicing and make sure your invoicing is automatic – not something that you have to do manually. When dealing with suppliers, use e-procurement if you can. Always check the terms you are being given – remember, a salesman may have told you that you will get special terms, but the finance department might not have added them on the order.

You also need to have policies for dealing with overdue payments. First of all, you will need to make your accounts system flag them up automatically. Then you'll need to decide what action to take. You might have several stages of action – first a reminder invoice, then a phone call, then sending the case to a debt collection agency, perhaps. Once you have set up your policy, stick to it.

Also, find out how your customers process invoices when they receive them. First of all, are you sending invoices to the right person in the organization.? If you are sending invoices to a purchasing manager it might not be that manager's priority to forward them to the accounts department – so make sure you have the right contact. If your customer has a monthly deadline and processes all payments once a month, don't miss the deadline when you are invoicing! If a customer needs a particular reference number included, ensure it is prominently featured on your invoice. Give as much information as possible about the order, so they don't have to waste time ringing up to check details.

It might seem that one way to help keep your working capital under control is to pay your suppliers as late as possible – but that can be counterproductive. Don't pay early, but make sure you pay exactly on time. If you make a habit of paying late, it is likely that suppliers will cut your terms of trade, giving you less credit, and even possibly refusing to supply you. If, on the other hand, you always pay by the due date and keep them happy, you will have a better relationship. That can mean that you can ask for a small order, or a rush job, and you may find you'll even get better terms, in the end.

One thing some stock market analysts have noticed is that it is often a very bad sign if companies aren't paying suppliers. Rather than showing that they are astutely managing their working capital, it suggests that their business models may not be viable, or their bank may be unwilling to give them further funding. It is surprising how many times a refinancing or even corporate failure follows a significant increase in payables.

Managing inventory is an art. Too many firms leave it to chance – they order when they find they have run out of something (too late) or always have a month's supply of everything (too much). Having too little inventory can mean you will lose sales, or lose production time when stock-outs stop the production line. Making orders that are too small can mean you miss out on bulk discounts and end up paying a higher price for your input costs than your competitors.

You may want to use the *safety stock* formula. It uses your maximum stock usage and average usage to determine what amount you need to keep in stock to meet fluctuations in demand and lead time.

(Maximum daily usage x maximum lead time) – (average usage x average lead time)

Of course, if you have pronounced seasonality, you might want to run a safety stock formula for peak season and a separate calculation for the rest of the year.

You will also want to set a reorder point that takes account of safety stock and of the lead time. For instance, if you are importing clothes from Tunisia, you will want to factor in manufacturing time (if the clothes aren't in stock), shipping time, time for customs clearance, and time for internal distribution – for instance, a retailer with multiple branches will need a couple of days to distribute from the logistics center.

Suppose you have 52 days usual lead time, you will need to cover 52 days' sales' worth of stock. You might look at that in terms of monetary value, or units of stock – say, we sell five dresses a day, then 52 days' worth of stock equals 260 dresses. Then, just to be safe, add your safety stock to that figure. That might be 150 dresses, so your reorder point would be 260 + 150 = 410 dresses in total. Quite simply, when you get down to 410 dresses in stock, you need to reorder.

The equation is the same for a manufacturer – you know how much of each component or raw material your process uses each day, you know what the lead time is for each component, and you know the variances (longest lead time, busiest production), so you can calculate a reorder point.

Setting reordering policies in place, and monitoring inventory levels regularly so that you are always in control, will help keep working capital at the optimum levels for your business.

Look for items of stock that aren't getting used, or aren't moving out of the shop. Try to set up automatic warnings in your accounts system for slow-moving stock. You should also think about whether any significant patterns are showing. For instance, one clothes retailer found that anything in red took longer to shift, *except* for shoes and handbags. In a small business, usually staff have a good feel for slow-moving stock, but the accounts are a good check on your gut feel.

Also look for stock-outs – stock that's gone to zero. That may be quite normal – the end of season sale at a fashion retailer, a decision to run down old stocks – but it might also occur on current stock, and the results can be considerable. It is most evident at retailers – for instance, where a supermarket runs out of a basic item, customers get grouchy, and the supermarket loses the sale – but manufacturers also have big problems with stock-outs.

For example, one craft brewer had a hard decision to make when she ran out of Cascade hops and couldn't get resupplied in time for the weekly brew – reschedule the brew (which meant paying part-time staff to come in for an extra day), or brew a different recipe which might not be so salable as the main-brand IPA? That is a case from a small business. In a larger manufacturing business, the outcome could be more serious. One fifty-cent component being out of stock could stop manufacturing at a plant turning out $50,000 cars.

Stock-outs can be particularly serious for businesses that provide an all-in-one or one-stop-shop service for complex assemblages of products. For instance, a fitted kitchens retailer that is out of one type of handle, and can't get resupplied, may face a customer deciding that if they can't get the handle they want, they will shop elsewhere. Builders' merchants and other trade suppliers know that their customers will arrive with a list of exactly the products and components they want – and expect to have those orders filled.

Have a system for recording all stock-outs and their operational results (disgruntled customer, lost sale, lost production). You will soon see where you have problems.

However, stock reduction isn't just about daily management. For best results, you need to look at the structural make-up of your inventories. For instance, reducing the number of different components stocked can make a big change to the amount you will need to keep. An oil and gas company could standardize from seven types of valve to just one – a strategic solution rather than just cutting stock levels. Keeping products standard until a later stage of production, and then customizing, can also help to reduce both raw materials and work in progress.

Sometimes a straightforward solution can work. One stationery shop kept seven different versions of each Pelikan fountain pen, one with each size of nib. There was a red M400 with italic nib, a green M400 with italic nib, a blue M400 with italic nib, and then the same three pens with a fine nib, with a medium nib, and a broad nib; 12 pens altogether, one of each. However, a student working there for the summer pointed out that the nibs were interchangeable, and could be bought separately – so all they needed was the pens together with a range of (much cheaper) spare nibs. If a customer wanted a combination they hadn't got, they could just swap nibs over.

Managing receivables is a bit of a black art, or at least you would think so when you see the number of businesses that can't seem to get to grips with it. Part of the job is just about fast and efficient invoicing, but there is also a more strategic level, which is about credit control.

You will need to think about customers' creditworthiness. Banks do this in a very structured way, using external credit reference companies and internal credit scoring systems. If you have corporate customers, you should check their financial statements and watch out for articles in the financial press to assess the level of risk you run in extending credit to them. But for many businesses, the best assessment of customers' creditworthiness is your experience. Keep track of each customer's record of payments; on-time? Always going to a reminder, but then paying up smartly? Or reordering without ever paying that first invoice?

While a one-off characterization of customers (good payer, grudging payer, problem payer) can be useful, keep an eye open for changes over time. If an on-time payer suddenly starts needing reminders, and one or two orders stack up without overdue payments being made, it is a signal that something's going wrong – you will need to take action, both to recover those late payments, and perhaps to trim back credit terms or even ask for cash payment.

Always work out your DSOs (days sales outstanding, calculated as overdue payments / revenue x days). While payables days measure your total credit extended to customers, DSOs measure the capital you have tied up in overdue invoices. If you see that figure rising, you need to work out why. If you have recently had a major sales drive, or gone into a new market, you might have picked up some problems on the way. Or you may not have been chasing overdue invoices hard enough. Or you might have one or two customers with real problems. The DSOs figure will be your best warning.

You may also want to take strategic decisions about how credit-worthy your customers need to be. Banks do this all the time – some will actively court sub-prime customers as a way to get higher returns or greater market share. For instance, you may find you can get good returns by targeting start-up companies for your products, and some consultants do well out of advising turnaround companies that have got into difficulties and need to make drastic changes to recover. Entering an export market might also deliver high sales growth but could involve higher risks of non-payment.

One way around the problem for exports markets is to insist on cash payment upfront. Many companies exporting to Russia in the early days of glasnost decided to supply for cash, some of them through wholesaler partners who would take over the job of recovering payments.

Overall, you will want to look at your *current ratio* and *quick ratio* to see whether your working capital management gives you enough headroom to manage any disruption.

Current ratio – current assets / current liabilities

Quick ratio – current assets less inventory / current liabilities

The current ratio for traditional manufacturers could be 2 or more; for retailers, it might be below 1, particularly for giants like Walmart, because their credit terms are heavily in their favor. While you will use the sales to working capital ratio to check how profitably you are deploying your funds (the higher the sales to working capital, the better), the current and quick ratios give you a feel for how resilient your business is. If your quick ratio is below 1, you might have difficulty paying your bills as they become due.

As so often, there is no right answer – managing your working capital is about striking the right balance for the business you are running.

Funding Working Capital

Most businesses start off funding their working capital with an overdraft facility. That seems reasonable – working capital is, in essence, short-term – but it can be ineffective in the long run. Although individual receivables are short-term in nature, your working capital as a whole will continue to need funding in the long term, and an overdraft may not be the most effective, or cheapest, way to do that.

Asset finance can be an attractive proposition for companies with high levels of sales on credit. Alternative lenders specializing in asset finance often have lower cost finance than banks, so it is worth checking out a few providers.

With invoice discounting, you use your receivables as collateral for a loan. Once you have raised an invoice, the discounter will advance 90% of the invoiced amount; once it is paid, you will get the rest, less a small fee. Unlike an overdraft or a fixed loan, invoice discounting will automatically adjust to an increase in your business.

Factoring is slightly different in that it is not a loan; instead, you sell your receivables to the factor, who is then responsible for collecting payment.

For very small businesses, PTP lending and even Kickstarter can be worth a look. For instance, if you have a new product in development and need to finance a build-up of stock ahead of the roll-out, Kickstarter can help both with finance and with marketing.

Chapter 8 – Hedging Your Bets

Financial management includes a particular specialism, *risk management*, that is becoming increasingly better known. It is the banking sector which has led the way, as events like the collapse of Baring Brothers, Lehman, and Bear Stearns, together with flash crashes and 'fat-finger' trading reverses, have shown the need for better control of risk in the financial world, but most businesses can benefit from a structured program of identifying, monitoring, and controlling risk.

First of all, you will want to identify the main financial risks to which your business is exposed. These might include:

• Interest rates – if you have high debts at variable rates, an increase in interest rates could damage your business.

• Currency – if you export your goods or services, or if you have input costs which are imported or the price of which reflects a foreign currency, then this could have a big impact on your profitability.

• Commodities – if your input costs include a commodity such as oil, steel or barley, you are exposed to a change in the price of this commodity on the markets.

As with any kind of risk, with financial risks you will want to find out the size of the risk – for instance, a travel agent with a small downtown office and an airline will both have energy costs, but in the case of the travel agent, heating is a tiny part of its bills, while the airline has a very substantial bill for fuel.

You then need to decide what to do about the risks. You might ignore them – if (like the travel agent's heating bill) they are not significant in the context of the business. You could mitigate the risk – for instance, by shifting some of your finance to fixed-term loans. Or you could *hedge* the risk in various ways. Almost all hedges have a cost, so you need to consider carefully the decision to hedge and whether it is worth it.

A very simple hedge is an inbuilt hedge. For instance, if you buy a distributor in an export market, and finance it with a loan in that country's currency, you have matched your costs and income, so effectively you have hedged your exposure.

However, there are various other ways to hedge which can make sense if you have a large exposure to an identifiable financial risk.

• You might fix your future price for a major commodity by buying futures. You enter into a contract to buy your raw material at a certain date in the future and for a certain price. You can do this privately ('over the counter') but there are also numerous exchanges like Chicago Board of Trade that offer traded, standardized futures contracts.

• With a future, you are obligated to buy the commodity on the contract date, so if the price moves the other way, you give up any gain you might have made. Instead, you could buy an option, which – as the name implies – gives you an option on whether to exercise it (buy the underlying commodity) or not. You will have to pay something for the option, just as you pay something for your home insurance.

• You might also buy a financial product that offsets an exposure. For instance, you can buy Exchange Traded Funds (ETFs) for metals, interest rates, or equity markets. One property developer worried that the market was entering a bubble, so decided to offset some of its risk by buying a *short* (inverse) real estate ETF. It sounds counter-intuitive – surely if you think property is going to tank, you would get out of the business? – but there is actually a sound rationale for it. The developer makes money not by holding property, but by transforming it – the business is about adding value. By hedging the property market price risk, the developer can protect itself from the risk it can't do anything about and concentrate on making money by adding value to the properties that it develops.

If you think this all sounds too complicated, think again. Many of these hedging instruments are available to private individuals and small companies – you don't have to be a major corporate or a bank to use them.

You will need to get yourself educated on pricing, and you'll need to set up a way of monitoring your hedge and setting up a *rolling hedge* – that is, ensuring that your hedge reflects any increase in exposure – but anyone with a good background in business or basic finance should be able to set up a hedge that will help protect the business against unexpected market risks.

Chapter 9 – Management Accounting

While financial accountants who sign off companies' audits are the most public face of the accounting profession, an equally important branch is *management accounting*. Financial accountants tend to look for right answers and compliance with accounting regulations; management accountants, on the other hand, are looking for the answers to questions about business strategy and operations, and accept that the answers could be ambiguous or multiple. Financial accountants are responsible to the shareholders, and management accountants are responsible to the management.

Perhaps you don't have a management accountant in your business. Even so, management accountants have developed a number of techniques for analyzing business problems that you can put to use.

One of the keys to management accounting is *contribution* – that is, sales price per unit less variable cost per unit.

Breakeven Analysis

How many units of product or service need to be sold to cover fixed costs. For instance, how many billable hours do consultants need to work to cover their office costs, insurance, marketing, and support staff salaries? Or how many ice creams do La Gelateria need to sell to pay for staff salaries, rent, and refrigeration?

Breakeven point = fixed costs / (Sales price per unit – *variable cost per unit)*

In the case of the ice cream parlor, a two-scoop cone sells for $4. The materials for that sale cost $1, so the contribution is $3. Suppose the shop pays $1,800 a month in rent, $2400 in salaries, and another $600 in energy, adding up to $4,800. The break-even point is 4800 / 3 = 1600 ice creams, or at least 53 a day. (By the way, have you spotted that we can boil down this equation to fixed costs / contribution per unit?)

Armed with that figure, you could visit an ice cream parlor that looks similar to the one you are thinking of setting up – a similar location and size, and a similar slice of the market, whether family/economy or 'foodie'/high margin – and get settled in for lunchtime. Eat an ice cream nice and slowly and note how many ice creams are sold. If the lunchtime trade doesn't get past 50, you know you are going to have a tough time breaking even; if the parlor is selling hundreds of ice creams, you have got a great chance of being profitable from day one.

Where break-even analysis doesn't work too well is when you have a lot of different products – unless you can group them into an average sale. For instance, a restaurant would work out what is the average meal (one starter, one main course, two beverages, perhaps) and create the break-even analysis on that basis.

Limiting Factor Analysis

Sometimes a business has a limiting factor. For example, an architectural practice can only handle as much work as it has staff hours available; the size of its bottling plant may limit a brewer – it could produce more beer, but it couldn't bottle it. Limiting factor analysis tries to find the most profitable way of using that limiting factor – which jobs should the architect take on? Which beers should the brewer produce?

First, you need to work out the contribution of different products. For instance, the architect may make more money per hour worked from working on refurbishment jobs than from complete new ground-up projects, and may make much less doing architectural drawings and modeling. The brewer's highest contribution beer is the best bitter, and next, the very strong IPA whose high price more than pays for the bigger grain bill and higher tax.

Next, you need to look at the contribution *per unit of the limiting factor*.

In the case of the brewer, all beers take the same time to bottle – if, on the other hand, the limiting factor was the fermenter, some beers take longer to ferment than others, so you would need to work out the contribution of the beer per day in the fermenter.

Again, if it is staff hours in general that the architects are short of, they don't need to go that extra step – but suppose it is one architect in particular who has a specialist who is the limiting factor because they can't handle any more work that needs his or her input? In that case, you will need to look at the best way of using that particular architect's hours, so a relatively low contribution job which only uses a small proportion of that person's time could rank ahead of a higher contribution job which needs them to work on it extensively.

Of course, if limiting factors keep getting in the way, you ought to think about whether you need to make changes. An obvious question for the brewer is whether you need to add bottling capacity. If a limiting factor has become a huge bottleneck, then capital investment could address that – in one carpentry shop, there was always a queue for the planer/thicknesser, while other machine tools often stood idle. Buying a new planer helped solve the problem and almost doubled the capacity of the workshop.

What about the architects? They could consider training up a junior member of staff in the limiting factor specialism, they could take on a new employee, or they could look at outsourcing some of the work – though all those ideas would need to be discussed with the relevant staff member; otherwise, they could end up with an even worse situation.

Purchase Price Variance / Selling Price Variance

Calculating the actual price achieved per unit against your predictions in the budget can show you whether you are getting a higher or lower price than you expected. This can be particularly useful when you have got a major promotion going on – did your BOGOF or three-for-the-price-of-two work out the way you expected, or has it made a big hole in your budget?

Calculating your purchase price variance will show whether you are buying smart, or whether the price of basic materials has moved against you.

Using Scenario Analysis

This is a lot simpler than it sounds. Forecast your sales and costs using your 'base case' – that might be 'the same as this year', or 'this year plus 3%', or it might be your first ideas, in the case of a start-up. Then start tinkering. Copy your spreadsheet onto a new tab and say, "Okay, I'm going to reduce the price by 10% and see if I can still break even. I'm going to see what happens if my sales are only half what I expected. I'm going to start with a smaller production facility and fewer staff – or a bigger one and double; what happens? What's the right decision?"

If you tinker with one set of numbers at a time – alter unit sales *or* prices but not both at once – you get a great idea of how the business might respond to particular actions. Scenario analysis might tell you that you need to start big and get economies of scale, or you won't survive – or it might tell you to start small and scale up. It might tell you that you can halve your price and still survive – or that you have a very, very limited room for maneuver.

Scenario analysis isn't going to give you a perfect forecast, and like many things, it is GIGO – garbage in, garbage out; you will only get the best out of it if you do some serious thinking about the scenarios you want to model. However, it's a fantastic way to structure your thinking around business and financial issues and to test your ideas before you put them into practice.

Chapter 10 – Ratios – Your Management Dashboard

When you are driving a car, you don't have a printout of all the different numbers involved. You have a visual display of speed, revs, and blinking lights to tell you about oil levels (if too low), headlights (on, dimmed, off) or if you are running low on petrol. In the same way, you need to build a management dashboard that can show you very quickly the main financial trends affecting your business.

One of the key ways to do this is to stop looking at the basic numbers and instead look at the ratios (what some accountants call 'vertical analysis' because you are comparing a number with another one further up or down the page, compared to 'horizontal analysis' which compares this period's figures with previous periods).

In this chapter, we are going to run through some of the most important ratios for analyzing your business.

Return On Sales

There are various ways you can calculate return on sales – your profit margin percentage. It shows how much profit you make on each dollar of sales. Gross profit margin is useful for retailers and other businesses which make a markup on materials. Businesses with a higher proportion of fixed costs probably want to look at operating profit or EBITDA margin. You may also want to look at post-interest and post-tax margins. Calculating these sums is simple – profit / sales x 100.

When you look at your return on sales, you need to compare it with other firms in your sector, as well as with your past figures. Are you getting better or worse returns than you did last year? Is there a long-term trend? Do you beat your competition, or are you less profitable? If you put in place a strategy for improving your profit margins, you will want to track it closely and make sure you achieve the desired effect.

Interest Cover

While you are looking at the profit and loss account, you should calculate interest cover, which shows how many times you can cover your interest bills with the profit that you make. The formula is simply operating profit / interest payable. If you only make enough profit to pay your interest, it would be 1 – and you would be in real trouble. Most businesses like to see interest cover at 2 or more – that means profits could halve, and they would still be able to pay the interest on their bank loans.

Returns On Assets / Investment / Equity

There is a slightly confusing wealth of ways to calculate these figures, but they all show, in various ways, how well you are making use of the business' assets (balance sheet) to make a profit. Analysts and management consultants can get very excited about how exactly each calculation is done, but from the point of view of a business manager, don't stress too much – the whole point of doing the ratios is to give yourself a basis of comparison, so as long as you are consistent, the exact detail doesn't matter too much.

ROCE or return on capital employed is calculated as EBIT / total assets minus current liabilities. It shows how much operating profit the business makes for each dollar of capital (both equity and debt) used. If two businesses make the same amount of profit and the same gross profit, but one of them uses twice the amount of capital to do so, then it is not as efficient as the other company – and it will need to invest twice the amount of new funds to get the same growth in profits. You should also compare ROCE to the cost of borrowing – if it is below the rate you are paying on debt, then you aren't making enough profit.

ROA or return on assets (sometimes referred to as ROI, return on investment) looks at net income (post interest and tax) as a percentage of total assets. You really need to track both figures – ROCE is more comparable across companies, while ROA will show you how efficiently your financial structure is set up.

Activity Ratios

We already looked at working capital ratios in the relevant chapter, but there are other activity ratios you need to look at to see how well your business is using your assets.

• Inventory turnover (cost of goods / average inventory) shows how quickly your stocks are being converted into cash.

• The overall turnover ratio (sales / total assets) shows how well assets are being used to create revenue.

Because activity ratios use turnover, not profit, you are looking at the basic efficiency of the process in turning over your assets. Of course, you will also want to look at the profit numbers – if you are getting high stock turnover by giving your goods away, that is not great news. But activity ratios will show you if your use of assets becomes less efficient, perhaps because your purchasing manager got some basic trends wrong this season, or because your production line is aging and has needed extra maintenance, which reduced production hours.

Making Your Management Dashboard

You will probably already have a feeling for which ratios are most important and give you the best information about your particular business. Remember that you might build in other stats as well, outside the strictly financial sphere – you might want to look at customer satisfaction, occupancy rates, or customer acquisitions. You can build all these stats into a single monthly report, and automate its production from your accounting software – it will be well worth your while, as every month, you'll have the key data laid out in a user-friendly way, and you can make efficient use of your time to decide how to take the business forward.

Here are a few examples of how the dashboard for different businesses could differ.

In each case, managers have asked for the selection of figures and ratios that will give them the best quick view of the business; they can then drill down into detail if they want to, or if some of the figures in the overview lead to questions about the reasons for changes, or about operational performance:

• A retail business would probably lead with the big picture – sales compared to historic data and budgets; gross margin; stock turnover. You might want to add the size of the average sale, to measure how well your staff is upselling extras.

• A capital-intensive business would probably want to prioritize activity ratios and return on assets / capital. Capacity utilization data might also be useful (was your plant working full time? Or only 76% of the time?).

• A services business would put billable hours and hours billed right up the top, together with profitability ratios. If there is not much capital in the business, there's not much point looking at ROCE and ROA. On the other hand, receivables could be very important in a business that is billing customers after the service has been provided (and after the staff has been paid).

Chapter 11 – A Quick Look At Risk Management

We already talked about hedging, but financial management should include a more general risk management function looking at risks from terrorism or fire destroying the premises through to network outages and basic human mistake. This is where financial and operational management needs to work together – but finance will be the guys putting together the figures.

In looking at risk, there are two myths you need to get rid of:

1. The myth that 'Risk is bad'. That is built into the way some people refer to 'risky' activities (bungee jumping, skydiving) or 'risky' investments (unprofitable companies, deep out-of-the-money options). In fact, risk can be good – if taking a small risk gives you a potentially large reward, it is worthwhile. The important thing is the risk/reward factor. You shouldn't reject a new business plan because 'it's risky', but only if the risk is larger and/or more likely than the potential reward.

2. The myth that only big risks are worth considering. To assess a risk, you need to multiply its severity (the money you'd lose) by its probability (the chance that it's actually going to happen). The risk that terrorists blow up your manufacturing plant is incredibly severe – but it is not very probable. On the other hand, the risk of a computer outage costing you an hour's production or sales may not be particularly massive in financial terms, but it is much more

probable – and if it happens a few times every month, it could represent quite a large risk for you overall.

So, first of all, you need to draw up a list of risks and evaluate both their financial impact and their probability. Don't forget liability risks – the building that develops a structural fault could raise a big liability case against an architect's firm, for instance.

You can then see what are the important risks and think about what action to take; the mantra is 'accept, transfer, mitigate, avoid' – four different ways of approaching a risk.

• Avoiding a risk might be sensible if, for instance, you have two possible ways to finish a piece of furniture, one using a carcinogenic chemical and the other one using natural oils. You might avoid the risk of competing for low margin public contracts where you could easily end up making a loss if your budgets aren't 100% on target.

• Mitigating a risk might be operational – using guards on machinery to avoid the risk of employees being injured, putting warnings on coffee cups so that customers don't sue you if they burn their mouths. Risk mitigation can try to reduce the probability of risk, or its severity – for instance, a laboratory could mitigate contamination risks by dividing up its space into airtight, non-communicating compartments so that even if one process goes wrong, it has no impact on the rest of the business. (Mind you, watertight compartments *didn't* work for the Titanic.)

• Accepting the risk is sensible if you need to do so to carry out the business, and you can make a contingency budget available. Many businesses *self-insure* for certain risks – effectively, it is the same decision as deciding that since you have enough cash to replace your luggage, you are only going to take out travel insurance that covers medical bills.

• Finally, transferring the risk might be done through an insurance policy (for instance, a premises insurance, or a liability insurance), or through hedging, or through outsourcing certain parts of the business. Many businesses set up joint ventures to handle business they consider represents an unacceptable risk.

You will also want to think about *contingency planning* and *emergency preparedness* (basically, special subsections of risk mitigation). If you have a major accident at your plant, how will you cope? How quickly can you get up and running again? Are you likely to face claims from neighbors whose premises were affected? Office-based businesses might think about how to react if access to their premises became difficult, perhaps through public transport strikes, perhaps because of an incident elsewhere in the building or on the road outside. Could staff work from home using a VPN? Could an alternative site be made available?

Risk management can also make you look at your financial ratios in another light. For instance, you can look at margins as your protection against risk. If you have high margins, you can accept a bit more risk in your customer credit control process, or a bit more risk in terms of higher funding from bank loans. Lower margins mean you will want to take less financial risk.

Management consultants BCG gave the example of First Solar, which reduced risk by manufacturing 'good-enough' solar cells – moderately efficient and very low cost. It could do so with relatively little capital expenditure or research and development spend. This policy let the company scale up and achieve profitability very fast compared to competitors – because it was funding development through cash flow, the 2008 credit crunch didn't hurt it as much as it damaged competitors who needed to raise loan finance. You might not go quite as far as this in your thinking – but it illustrates how, just like financial management, risk management can go beyond box-ticking and budget-making to transform the strategy of a business.

Conclusion

This book has taken a very fast gallop through a very complex sphere of operations. None the less, if you have made it to the end, you should now have a good grasp of how financial management works – even if you prefer to leave the details of some aspects to your finance department.

Not every business will need every aspect we have covered. Some businesses may not have major exposures that need hedging; some businesses will not have limiting factors, or will not have extensive inventory to manage (one graphic designer described her stock as 'five bottles of ink and a desk drawer full of paper', which probably doesn't require accounting software to manage). However, whether you need individual weapons or not, you should now have a full armory.

You could stop here. Instead, we are going to suggest that right now, while the subject matter is fresh in your mind, you make notes on between three and five ways you could apply financial management techniques to your business to improve your financial returns. They may be very simple; if you are a start-up and you have never run proper budgets, this could be time to start. You might want to analyze your cost of capital and see if you can drive down the cost of borrowings. You might want to work on improving your return on assets or think about hedging a large exposure to oil prices. Whatever it is, jot it down, and when you have done it, assess how much contribution it made to your business and how you can improve even more.

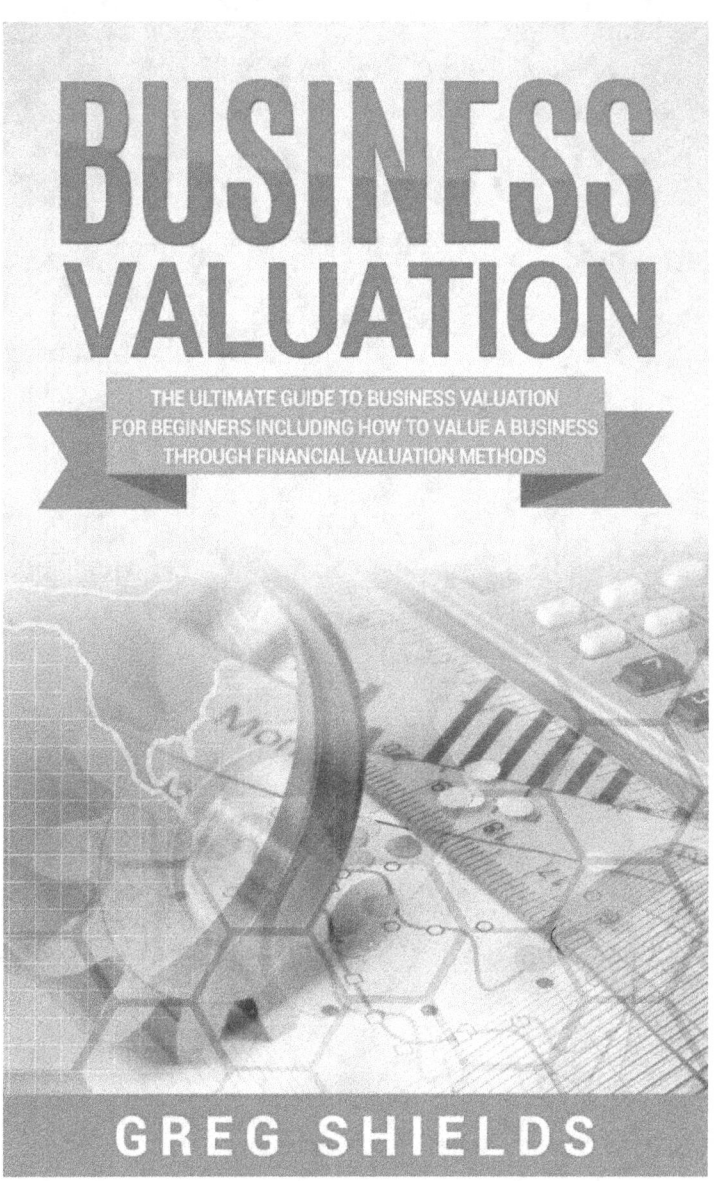

Check out this book!

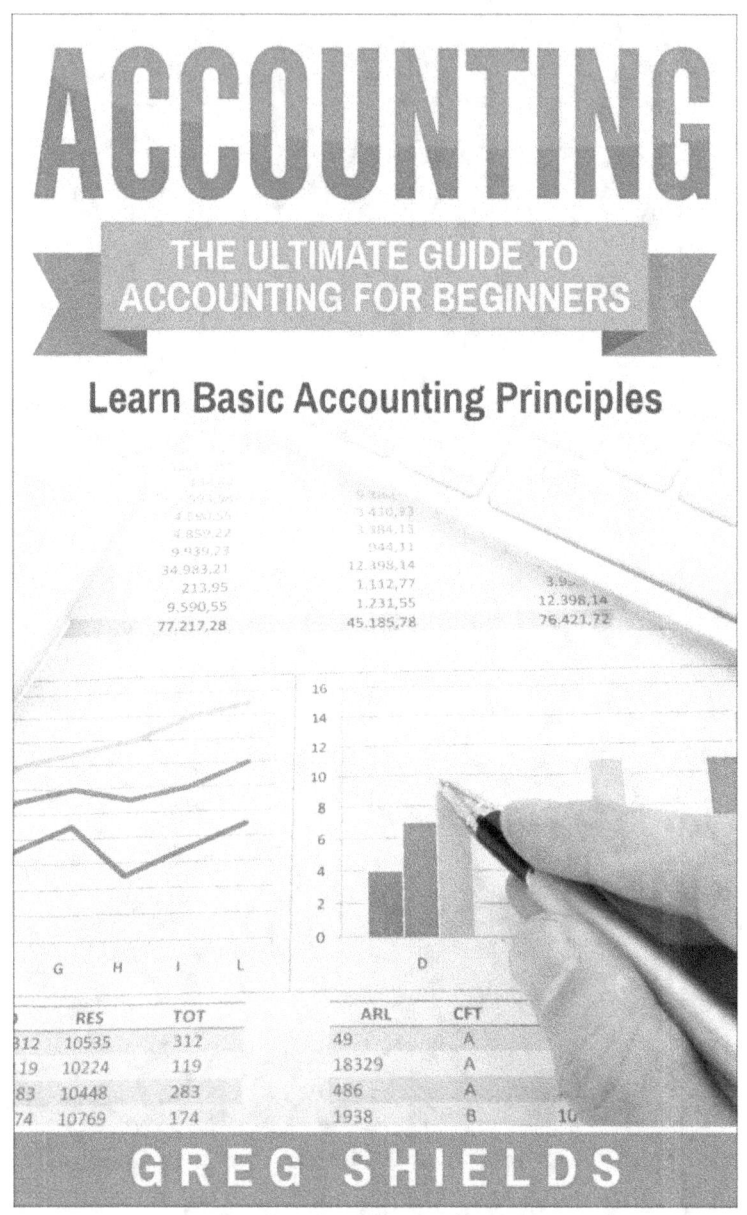

Check out this book!

Check out this book!

Resources / Sources of Information

The non-profit sector has some really good resources for financial management, perhaps because it is an area at which many non-profits are rather weak – when you are fighting for a cause, finance might not be top of your mind.

https://fcyo.org/resources/financial-management-resource-toolkit has references to easy-to-use, open-access resources on the web. It even includes a financial dashboard custom-made for non-profits.

https://knowhownonprofit.org/organization./operations/financial-management/management

There is a neat study package here for managers in non-profits. 'Finance is too important to be left to the honorary treasurer' the site says, a sentiment with which we heartily agree.

The Institute of Chartered Accountants (ICAEW) has some splendid resources on its website, including a guide to financial management for SMEs (**https://www.icaew.com/-/media/corporate/archive/files/about-icaew/what-we-do/policy/budget-and-pbr/final-bis-smes-financial-managementnew.ashx**) with links to other sources of advice.

There are a number of books that can take your appreciation of financial management further. For risk management, you might enjoy reading some of Nassim Nicholas Taleb's work, particularly *The Black Swan*, which looks at how to cope with extreme, unpredictable events. It is written for a general public and is extremely thought-provoking.

Gene Sicilliano's *Finance for non-Financial Managers* goes through all the basics in great detail, with plenty of examples. However, you may find you already know most of what is in it.

On the other hand, if you are looking for a reference book and an introduction to more in-depth analysis of financial concepts, you will probably want to get to grips with Edward Fields' *Finance and Accounting for non-Financial Managers*. It will take you through an intensive education in how to read balance sheets, analyze profit and loss accounts, and put together an annual report. But it is pretty hard work. And it's a little bit biased towards the financial accountant's job rather than the management accountant's.

Droms & Wright's *Finance and Accounting for non-Financial Managers* covers the same material, but its core strength is the case studies it contains and the depth of its treatment. This would be our favorite of the three general finance books.

Most news media give 'financial news' in snippets that don't contain much, if any analysis, or that are orientated towards investors rather than managers. However, there are some good media that you should read for a more considered and in-depth reportage.

FEI Daily (**https://daily.financialexecutives.org**) is aimed at financial controllers and finance officers. Stories recently have included looking at the impact of Blockchain on finance, how to manage IT spend, and detailed advice on building more accurate forecasts and budgets.

Barrons (**www.barrons.com**) is aimed at investors but often carries in-depth discussions of financial trends in industry sectors or across the market. It is a nice corrective to getting bogged down in accounting detail – finance as a strategic discipline is what Barrons is all about. Additionally, if you are of a size where raising money from the public markets is appropriate, the magazine will give you a great feel for market sentiment.

The Wall Street Journal's CFO Report (**https://blogs.wsj.com/cfo/**) and the Wall Street Journal's business news hide behind a paywall – but may well be worth your paying for. However, coverage isn't always as in-depth as Barrons.

Don't overlook the rich resources that the big accountancy firms put out for their clients and the public at large. KPMG (**https://home.kpmg.com/xx/en/home.html**), PWC (**https://www.pwc.com/us/en.html**), Deloitte (**https://www2.deloitte.com/us/en.html**) and EY (**https://www.ey.com**) all have significant free resources; however, you may need to put a little work into learning your way around the websites to make the best use of them. Bookmark parts of the site that are most useful to you, such as relevant sector teams' pages. Often, the website will lead with a few take-aways from a story but let you download a full report on the subject as a PDF – these can be full of interesting insights and quite often have startling details (for instance, on automation; one investment bank has replaced 600 equity traders with a computer program and just two actual traders – an amazingly radical result).

The Small Business Administration has a financial program for small businesses available on **https://www.sba.gov/blogs/free-training-resources-**

financial-management-available-small-business-owners; the Learning Center is also worth perusing for courses on many topics, not just finance, many delivered through both video and workbooks.

There are some great blogs around, too. Bluevine (**https://www.bluevine.com/blog/?pid_login=0000586**) has regular posts detailing how to get business financing with a strong suit in asset finance, while accounting cloud software provider Freshbooks has a blog covering all kinds of small business topics but with a strong finance aspect, as you would expect (**https://www.freshbooks.com/blog/**).